WILL WRITING

WILL WRITING

How To Write A Will Easily

Neil Hurst

Table of Content

vi

Chapter 1 - About Wills

A will is a declaration made by a testator, the person making the will. In its legal form, it means that the person simply states what he wants to take effect upon his or her dead. Simply put, it is the last wishes of a person once they have passed on.

The old adage "when there's a will, there's a way" is something which really applies in this context. Applied to will making, it seems to pave the way for a person's property to be distributed according to their wishes and a simple instruction to others as well.

This book is a guide for simpletons who wish to understand what Wills are. If you are someone who is considering having a will (which everyone should have) this guide gives you the basic information you need. It doesn't cover your local legislation, however. This is general information for someone wanting to know more about will writing.

What Are The Characteristics Of A Will

In the making of Wills, most legislation around the world prescribes to these characteristics. I can't speak for all countries, but I have never heard of any laws in a country that break these characteristics of a will. These are the general characteristics of a will.

(1) Wills Operate As A Declaration Of Intention

This means that even if you have created your will, you would still have the freedom to dispose your property or other ownership during your lifetime. This isn't like a sort of contractual agreement which only takes effect when there are parties signing the document.

A will would not affect your power to dispose your assets should there be a need for it. As an example, if you have a plan to leave your estate to your son if you die but decide to sell it instead, you can do so. Your son wouldn't be "receiving" it under the will, although there hasn't been a formal revocation of the will.

In this book, a very common term that you would hear is the executor. An executor is a person which is appointed by the will maker to administer a person's estate should he die. Unless there is a valid objection, the judge would appoint the person named in the will as the executor. You would learn more about executors in the following chapters.

Another fact is that the executor of a deceased's estate has the power to sell the property which is subjected to a specific gift. If during the course of the administration of the estate, it is found out the said estate has been sold or that the deceased residuary estate is not sufficient to absorb the liabilities of the estate, the beneficiaries would not be entitled to the gifts specified in the will.

(2) Wills Are Not Merely Confined To Property Disposal

It is commonly thought that the most important function of a will is to dispose of your property. This is true, but there are also other important functions of having a will.

Wills can be used to revoke all the earlier Wills, appoint guardians to take care of your children who are still minors in event that they are orphaned and appoint specific individuals to perform specific tasks. These specific tasks include appointing executors or trustees; and conferring them special powers to ensure the continuity of your business or how you wish your assets be distributed.

You could also add in directives about how you want to be burial or cremation, if you wish to use your organs for medical transplants or research. You could also leave loving terms of endearment to your loved ones if you died untimely.

(3) Wills Must Be In The Prescribed Form

For a Will to be in effect, it has to comply with the formal requirements as laid down by the law. This states that it should be in writing, be it handwritten, typewritten or printed. It could be in any language.

For it to be effective, the testator must sign or affix his signature or thumbprint at the end of the will. It should be placed in such a way that it becomes obvious that it was intended to ensure that the writing of the will is effective.

A Will also needs to be witnessed by a minimum of two people present during the timing of the signature of the will by the testator himself or the person who is signing on his behalf. This signature could also be acknowledged by the testator to the two witnesses in their presence, as the signature to his will. Each witness would sign in the testator presence and in the presence of each other.

(4) A Will Takes Effect Only Upon Death

As a will would only take effect upon the death of the testator, the beneficiaries and executors have no power or rights on the estates until the testators is dead. Therefore, a will is capable of dealing with properties or assets acquired after the date it was made.

For example, if you have stated clearly in your will that you want to split all the shares you have invested in the stock market equally among your children, and if your acquire any extra shares after the date of the will, the new shares would be included in the will as well.

(5) A Will Is Revocable

A will could be revoked before the testator's death. He may choose to do it voluntarily or because of certain events which happen. These are the situations which would revoke a will:

- **Writing A New Will** - This is perhaps the most common form of will revocation. From time to time, how we want our estates to be distributed would change. We may also decide to change the content of our Wills because of our change in beliefs. The rule in will writing is that a later will would always supersede earlier Wills which are being made. Therefore, it is a common thing that all Wills should be dated properly to avoid confusions and dispute in the future.

- **Marriage** - If a person is single during the time of will writing, the will would automatically be revoked the moment he gets married. If there are plans for him to get married in the future, he could state that his will would take into consideration of his future marriage to a particular person.

The name of the future spouse should be clearly stated in the will. If this is done properly, the will would remain valid even after marriage. This rule is applicable to both men and women.

- **Destruction** - If a will is destroyed with an intention of revoking it, it would be considered revoked. However, this would not constitute an effective will revocation if there is an accidental destruction or destruction by a third party. A copy of the original will can be accepted by court if it could be proven that the original has been destroyed without the testator's intention of revoking the will.

- **Execution In Writing** - The testator could declare in clear writing of his intention to revoke his will of a certain date and put his signature on a piece of paper in the presence of two witnesses. The witness would attest to his signature, similarly to the procedure of writing a will.

Chapter 2 - Why Anyone Should Have A Will

This is something that many people always ask over and over again - Should I have a will? The answer is simple - unless you are immortal, you should definitely have a will. These are among the reasons of having a will.

(a) Protect Your Loved Ones And Your Assets

Having a Will allows you to decide on the people who would benefit from your estate and the portion which you want them to receive. If there isn't a Will, your estate would be distributed according to the legal provisions and people who are dependent on you may not be able to receive anything. Therefore, a will would greatly ensure your family's needs are met in the future.

(b) Minimizes Hassles

There are very few people who realize how difficult it is when losing someone. Added is the aggravation from the bureaucracy and red tape because of the intestacy (dying without having a will). If you die without a will, you would cause a lot of problems for the living.

In many situations, it may take several years before everything could be settled. If you have a will however, the Grant of Probate could be obtained within a year's period. Therefore, having a will helps to minimize the hassles that your loved ones go through to ensure that your assets are distributed smoothly.

(c) The Exercising Of Your Right

Many people fail to realize that writing a will is a right by itself. It is something which is allowed by law. When you have a will, you are able to appoint an executor to handle your affairs after you have died. Besides that, the guardian of your choice can be appointed for children for are still considered minors.

(d) Flexibility And Control

When writing a will, you won't give up on your assets as the will would only be effective upon your death. As such, you are still in control as you could easily draw up another new one to supersede the previous one.

Chapter 3 - The Dangers Of Not Having A Will

Not having a Will is a very troublesome thing that the living would have to suffer. If you are someone with any form of estate or assets whatsoever, having a Will helps a lot. You may not realize it is, but you definitely will understand the reasons for having it once you realize the dangers of NOT having one.

(1) Your Estate Would Be Distributed According To Law

If a person dies intestate (without a Will), the law naturally takes control of the person's estate. According to this, the estate would be distributed according to the law in the country. What this means is that the local law would determine who should inherit the estate and in the right proportion among the beneficiaries.

Regardless, the law would determine how and to who your estates would be distributed. This depends on the legal system in the different countries. However, with a binding will, the beneficiaries' right can be easily determined.

(2) You Would Need Letters Of Administration

Should there be intestacy, you would need letters of administration for the purpose of your estate administration. This is needed because an administrator would need to be appointed to manage your estate and distribute your assets according to the letter of the law.

Before someone could be an administrator, he or she has to obtain the consent of all beneficiaries before being allowed to act. It may be a very long period because it is extremely difficult to decide on an administrator who is agreeable to all beneficiaries.

(3) No Protection To People Unrecognized By Law

There are a certain group of people who are generally not recognized by law. This includes partners (unmarried), stepchildren and aged relatives. As they are generally not recognized in law, without having a will, their interests would not be protected as there isn't a special provision which caters to their needs.

(4) Abscondment Risk

The risk of abscondment happens when the administrator runs away with your estate. There have been such cases when Wills are not made. In such a situation, the sureties would need to bear the responsibility of refunding the loss.

****

From these four reasons, it is clear that having a will is very important. At times, not having a will would mean that it is even worse than not leaving anything for your loved ones. Without having a will, your estate may be a form of liability for your loved ones.

Chapter 4 - The Various Types of Wills

There are various types of Wills that you would need to know of before you start writing one. All of them have different purposes and you would need to be clear about them before making yours. They include:

(1) Individual Wills

This is the most common form of Will. This Will has to be written individually because each individual have different needs which has to be expressed in a different manner.

(2) Joint Wills

Joint Wills are made when there are two or more people who state their final wishes in a single document which is executed in accordance to the formalities of the law. Generally, a joint will wouldn't take effect as a single will. It is considered separate of the parties who have made it.

If a husband and wife decide to make a joint will and the husband was to die beforehand, the document would be admitted to probate first as the will of the husband upon death and secondly as the will of the wife after her death. It is not recommended to have a joint will as there would be confidentiality issues when the will of the person who dies first is lodged in court for probate.

(3) Mutual Wills

Mutual Wills are Wills made by two or more people who have an agreement between them to make such a will. Besides that, they also undertake an agreement to not revoke the will without the other party or parties consent. Normally, the terms of a mutual will would confer mutual benefits between the parties.

The principle of law when it comes to Wills is that a person can revoke his or her will any time before death. However, if one or more parties to a mutual will dies, leaving the other party as the sole survivor, the individual could revoke the mutual will but may find himself or herself liable for a breach of contract or trust.

(4) Living Wills

Living Wills (also known as advanced medical directive) are a written statement made by a person to direct doctors who are treating him in a terminal illness situation. He may state that he would want to discontinue treatment if it would only artificially prolong his life.

Chapter 5 - Who Should Write A Will

As you gain an insight as to what a Will is and why it is important, the next question that you should ask is: "Should I write a will".

YES! Of course, you need a will.

A lot of time when I talk to other people about Wills, their perception is that they belong to a group of people who don't need a will. Among the reasons include:

- They don't have a lot of properties or assets.
- They would only write a Will when they have more money or when they get rich.

These are not wrong perceptions but it is also subjected to a person's social and financial standing. As a matter of fact, if you are not rich and have dependents, writing a will may even be more important as you want your dependents to get your assets as soon as possible. This is especially so if you have money in the bank which would be frozen until a letter of administration is obtained.

If you were to take a look at your belongings, you would most likely find that you do own something. Most people have at least a few things in their name; from their savings, fixed deposit, unit trusts, car or even a small house. Those who have minors may even need to appoint someone they could trust to take care of their assets.

As such, it cannot be doubted that anyone with anything to their name should serious consider writing a will as soon as possible.

Chapter 6 - The Purpose Of Drawing Up A Will

From the previous few chapters, you should have a clearer picture about what a will is and why it is incredibly important of having one. In this chapter, you would learn about the actual purpose of drawing up a will. You would also learn about the various untold benefits from having a will properly written.

Among the purposes include:

(1) It Allows You To Understand Your Financial Planning Picture

Drawing up a Will allows you to initiate your own financial planning. When you draw up a Will, you would have a rough idea of the values of the assets that you have currently. To ensure that your loved ones inherit those assets, the best way is to write a Will. This would complete the financial planning picture.

As you write a Will, you would have completed the mission of allowing your loved ones to inherit your estate should anything happen. Writing a Will ensures that you have done a great job because you have covered yourself adequately with insurance and the planning of your wealth. As such, unconsciously, you have drawn up a financial plan as well as a proper estate distribution plan.

(2) Helps You Unlock Frozen Assets In A Shorter Period

Without a doubt, many people have certain dependents whom are partially or wholly dependent on them. This may include parents, spouse and children. They are dependent on the money they provide.

Can you imagine what would happen to them if the flow of money suddenly stops for them? It would cause a lot of difficulties for them. Therefore, it is important that you have proper instructions being left as to how the money would be accessible to the people in the quickest time available.

(3) Wills Are Unlimited

A Will which is written well would not be invalid even if your assets or estate grow over the years. Make sure that your Will is worded comprehensively and covers for such increases. If such, you wouldn't need to rewrite your Will every now and then. You would also ensure that the future assets that you purchase would be protected by Will.

This also increases the need to write a Will even when you are young and without any substantial assets. You don't have to worry that your assets in the future that you purchase would need a brand new Will. Of course, you could still update your Will, but you don't have to worry about doing it because a Will covers all your future assets, if written properly.

(4) Have Peace Of Mind

The moment you have written your will, you can have some peace of mind as you have made the appropriate arrangements for the distribution of assets to ensure that your beneficiaries are provided for. The most important thing is that you would be in control of your assets.

(5) It Is Cheap To Write A Will

When compared to other ways of preparing for the eventuality of death, writing a will is much cheaper. Just by paying for it one-time, you would be able to last as long as you don't revoke or write a new one.

If you decide to rewrite your will after a few years, the costs is minimal compared to the benefits and protection that you and your loved ones would enjoy. Among all the financial services available in the market, Will writing is a very cheap.

Chapter 7 - What A Will Would Generally Contain

For a Will to be effective, there are certain clauses or items that must be apparent. They are important because it allows the Will to be effective. Among the various items include:

(1) An Opening Clause

In every Will, there should be first stated an opening clause in which you identify yourself. If you have an alias or known by another name other than your given name (in your identity card), you should state that clearly in your Will. The opening clause also would include the date in which the Will is made. As stated in the previous chapters, a later Will would take precedence over any other Wills made earlier.

(2) Revocation Clause

Immediately after the opening clause, there would have a revocation clause where you state explicitly that you revoke any other earlier Wills which you have made. If you got married, it should be noted that this automatically revokes a Will unless the Will has include a contemplation of your marrying a particular person and a clause is added to that effect.

(3) Executors Appointment

The next thing that you would need to consider is to appoint an executor to the Will. This executor would be responsible to administer the deceased's estate upon death.

You may appoint up to four executors but it is often advisable to appoint more than a single executor. This is to ensure that there is a substitute in the event that the appointed executor dies before the testator or the executor has reached a stage where he or she is unable to perform the duties of an executor.

In a Will, the choice of executor or executors is perhaps the most important. Ideally speaking, you should appoint someone that you can trust. However, you should also make sure that they are willing to act on behalf on you before you appoint them in your Will. It should be noted that being an executor is a very demanding task as a lot of pressure can be put by the beneficiaries of the will.

Upon the death of the testator, if there isn't an executor who has the capability or is willing to act, or if the executors have predeceased the testator; a letter of administration with a Will annexed would need to be applied instead of a probate. This would be granted to such a person or persons as the court deems fit to administer the estate.

This procedure is similar to applying for letter of administration. The only difference is that the deceased's estate would be distributed according to the law of intestacy.

To avoid such a complicated situation, a trust corporation can be appointed instead. Trust corporations wouldn't die, become incapable or unwilling to act. Furthermore, the estate administration would be much smoother given the professionalism of such a trust corporation.

(4) Trustee Appointment

If you have children who are too young and cannot be trusted with too much money, a trustee could be appointed. The testator can choose to confer other powers of his trustees as well which are usually not provided under the letter of the law. This includes the power to carry on their business after his death or to invest in certain projects beyond what is commonly authorized by the law.

There are also other powers which you might want to confer upon your trustee for the purpose of managing your estate. These matters would need to be discussed with your personal lawyer or a professional Will-writer.

(5) Appointment Of Guardians

Guardians are people who you appoint for your children who are still minors. Guardians are responsible for protecting and providing for your children if you and your spouse were to die at the same time. Like executors, you should always ask for their permission first. You wouldn't want someone to agree initially but fail to perform his or her tasks if an unfortunate incident happens.

(6) The Distribution Of Assets

There could also be specific instructions on the type of gifts which are to be distributed and to whom those gifts are to be distributed and in what proportions. To ensure that those arrangements are made correctly, you should seek for someone with experience. Seek someone with professional expertise when it comes to Wills. Although many people think that lawyers would be the right people, it is better to seek a professional Will writer. Refer the back resource for a great online tool.

(7) Residuary Clause

This residuary clause is normally included to dispose any assets that you didn't dispose specifically in the Will. If there isn't such a clause, your possessions would be distributed according to intestacy laws and your wishes may not be fully realized.

(8) Specific Instructions

Before you dispose your estate, you could also leave certain specific instructions in your Will. This may be certain things that you want done after your passing which includes if you want to be buried or cremated, funeral arrangements or where you want your ashes to be placed.

Additionally, you would also want to include personal messages to your loved ones and beneficiaries. These messages are known as

"Terms Of Endearment" and could include religious connotations and prayer, certain advice to them or simply loving words to your family members.

This is a great method of leaving a lasting memory on your loved ones as there have been many cases where a person may suddenly passed on without having the opportunity to say anything to their loved ones or family members. These words would do great things to ensure that your loved ones remember you and ensure them that you still care for them.

(9) Testamentary Trust

Besides leaving instructions on how you want your assets to be distributed, there could be certain situations where you would want your assets to be distributed over a certain period of time. This may be because your beneficiaries may not be old or experienced enough to handle such a large amount of money.

In such a case, it is normally recommended to set up a testamentary trust in the Will. State clearly the instructions as to how you want those assets to be distributed and over the period. As you stagger the distribution in whatsoever combination you desire, you would eliminate the fear that the money would be squandered or lost over a period of time.

Review And Updating Your Will

A Will only takes effect upon the death of the testator. However, he or she may have acquired more properties, shares or have more money in the bank. There could also be situations where beneficiaries have died or may have other beneficiaries which you would want to consider. This may include your grandchildren.

It should also be clear that in the event of a separation or divorce, it wouldn't revoke a Will. Therefore, it helps to update your Will when there are certain major changes in your life, including financial or social changes. This is done by simply writing a new Will.

Chapter 8 - The Basics Of Will Writing

When it comes to Will Writing, it is always better to seek professional assistance. This helps to ensure that all those areas are addressed properly and avoid ambiguity when your Will is being read out to the beneficiaries.

This is important as the deceased definitely cannot be resurrected to give testimony of what he or she wants to say. Therefore, it is important that the Will be written well to ensure that there wouldn't be any doubt or conflicts. To ensure that a Will is written properly, there are certain information or formalities that should be followed before it could be considered valid.

(1) A Statement That The Testator Is Of Sound Mind

When the testator is making the Will, he or she should be of sound mind. Being of sound mind means that the testator should be clear about what he or she is doing. The testator should be clear that he or she is disposing his/her assets.

It is common practice that when the testator is writing his or her last Will on the deathbed, it is advisable to have a professional doctor to be one of the witnesses. This doctor would have the proper expertise to decide if the testator is of sound mind. Should the Will be contested subsequently in court, the doctor could be called upon to give his evidence that the testator is indeed of sound mind.

(2) The Age Of The Testator

This differs in various countries, but the minimum age of the testator is different. However, the general rule in most countries is 18 years old.

(3) The Will Must Be In Writing

The Will needs to be in writing and could be either handwritten or typewritten. An oral Will isn't sufficient unless it is a Privileged Will.

Privileged Wills are Wills which are made orally by mariners at sea, soldier or airman. They are normally employed in an expedition or engaged in actual warfare. However, there is still a minimum age requirement.

(4) Signature Or Affixation As An Execution

The testator would have to affix or sign his or her mark towards the end of the will. If the testator is unable to do it (in certain cases where the person is paralyzed or blind) someone could sign on his or her behalf.

(5) Attestation

To ensure that a Will is valid, it should be attested by two witnesses who are present during the time the testator signs or affix his or her mark.

The attestation by these two witnesses would also apply in certain circumstance when the testator is unable to sign and someone else signs for his or her behalf. A very important point to note is that the beneficiaries in the

Will and his or her spouse wouldn't be able to attest the Will or be its witness.

If this happens however, it doesn't mean that the entire Will is invalid. Only the provision that is invalidated is the gift that the witness is supposed to inherit under the Will. This rule is important as it prevents the likelihood of the beneficiary exerting undue pressure on the testator. Before any Will is being attest, make sure that you or your spouse isn't named as beneficiaries in the Will.

Witnesses of a Will wouldn't need to know the contents of the Will. What they are simply attesting is the testator's signature and acknowledges the fact that the testator is of sound mind and not under any undue influence when signing on the Will.

Chapter 9 - How To Draw Up A Will

The process of drawing up a Will is a simple process once you understand all the different issues involved. Before you start, these are certain points that you should consider:

(1) Are You Seeking Professional Help?

In legal terms, anyone could write a Will but it is better to seek help from a professional to ensure that you have dealt with all the relevant issues in a proper manner. This reduces the possibilities that your Will would be contested in court - a situation that would be very troubling for the beneficiaries. This could frustrate your intended plans in your

Will and make it very difficult for your loved ones in the future.

(2) Who Do You Want As Your Executors?

This is perhaps the first issue that you should consider. Your executor is the most important person in your Will as he or she would determine whether your Will is actually applied.

The executor is responsible to administer your estate. This means that he or she would manage your affairs when you have passed on. You could appoint up to a maximum of four executors but only one executor is needed to administer your estate.

In general practice, most professional Will writers recommend appointing more than one as this would provide an alternative arrangement should something unfortunate happen to an executor. If something do happen to the single executor, it would be hard for your Will to be executed.

The choice of who to be your executor is important. You should ask yourself as to who in your life is honest and reliable. He or she should also be responsible and willing to give his or her time to perform the tasks of administration your estate.

If you find someone who is capable of doing so, you would also need his or her consent before appointment. You may even appoint one of your beneficiaries as your executor of the Will. If you do have trouble finding an executor, a trust corporation can also help you.

(3) Do You Need To Appoint Guardians?

If you children are still minors during the time of writing your Will, a guardian or guardians should be appointed. In the event that you die but your spouse survives, he or she can fulfill the role of the guardian.

However, if a spouse predeceases the testator or both of them were to die together, it is advisable to entrust someone with the task of taking care of your children. The guardian will have children custody and responsible for their health, support and education.

(4) Who Are Your Beneficiaries?

This is something that you should really take some time to consider. Who do you want to benefit from your Will? You could have as many beneficiaries as you want but if you decide to leave your entire estate to a sole beneficiary, you should have an alternative. This is to ensure in certain situations where the sole beneficiary predeceases you.

(5) How You Want Your Estate Distributed?

In addressing the contents of your Will, you should decide what you want to leave every beneficiary. This includes any assets like your jewelry, car, house, money, stocks and shares. However, it should be noted that your liabilities aren't transferable. Besides leaving your estate to beneficiaries, you could also leave a legacy by donating it to charitable organizations or other non-profit organizations.

Chapter 10 - Ensure That The Will Is In Safe Custody

As you have your Will drawn up, a very important thing to consider is to where you should keep your Will to ensure its safety. Keeping your Will safe is important as there would be certain information that you would want to ensure that are private and confidential. Among the main two questions to consider include where to keep your will and who to keep it for you.

(1) Where Do You Keep Your Will

Wills have to be kept safely as it is vital so you are able to ensure that is kept well and thus the confidentiality of its content is being preserved. You wouldn't want other people to see your Will and try to tamper it.

If you keep it by yourself, you should let certain trustable people such as your executors know where it is. If you are dead, the Will could be located or retrieved for the application of probate. In general, most testators would decide to keep their Will in a bank safe deposit box or a secret location which nobody knows.

Under such situations, there are certain difficulties involved because upon death, the deceased's safe deposit box would be frozen and the Will wouldn't be able to be taken out. On the other hand, if the location is so secretly kept that no one knows, the Will wouldn't be located and having the Will would be useless.

(2) Who Should Keep It For You

As you consider the question above and try preventing any loss from happening, the Will should be kept by someone else. However, in such a case, you should always choose someone you have complete trust over to ensure that the content of the Will wouldn't be disclosed.

Additionally, it should also be kept securely to ensure any accidental or deliberate tampering or destruction of the Will cannot be done. This arrangement may seem feasible in the beginning but there isn't any guarantee that the Will could be located. The person might have misplaced the Will or predeceased you. Should such a case happen, the purpose of writing the Will is lost as well.

Using Professional Will Custody Services

To prevent tampering and destruction to your will, a more complete system of safe keeping and ease of retrieval needs to be arranged. As there has been an increase in the important of Will writing, the need for professional safe custody service becomes necessary. Because of this, some companies have offered Will custody services and they have various benefits. Among them include:

- **Free From Tampering** - As no one would have access to the Will you have wrote, the fear of tampering with the Will could be eliminated and this would definitely give you a peace of mind.

- **Protect From Destruction** - When you ensure that your Will is safe from potential destruction, you would feel better. Being kept in a strong Wills which only has Wills would ensure that your Will is safe from many natural disasters like floods, burglary or accidental/deliberate destruction.

- **Kept In A Secure Location** - As you Will is being kept by a corporation, it could be easily located because it is centrally kept at a permanent location. These professional Will custody services have appropriate functions that help ensure that you will is safe.

- **Controlled Access And Confidentiality** - All professional Will custody services would have a system of personal identification cards and a proper retrieval procedure. This helps prevent your Will from being exposed. Only you would have access to your Will during your entire lifetime or your executors upon death. Therefore, confidentiality is preserved once again.

- **A Personalized Service Just For You** - These professional services would contact you on an annual basis and may offer other services like giving up updates on changes in law or other relevant financial services. Other services may include financial planning tools to organize your assets or updating your assets inventory. In the future, your executors wouldn't need to go through a 'treasure hunt' in order to locate your assets while administrating them.

- **Free Insurance** - Unknown to many, this is actually free insurance as well. Certain corporations have enhanced services of providing free personal accident insurance to those testators who keep their Wills with them.

It is clear that there are various problems if you don't keep your Will well. Judging by this, it is important to know that writing your Will is only one part of the problem. There is another part of it and that is to keep the document safe on one side. Therefore, you should always find a Professional Will Custody Services.

Chapter 11 - Deciding On Your Personal Representatives

In the context of law of succession, "personal representation" refers to both the executor and administrator of the deceased's estate. You should always remember that.

(1) Executor

An executor is a person or corporate body (trust corporation) that specializes in the management of the affairs of the estate or other trust matters. The rights and duties conferred to a trust corporation is similar to an ordinary personal representative as they have to abide by all the requirements set about by the law, including the rules set about by the courts.

As stated in previous chapters, when appointing a person as executor, the testator may appoint a single person or more. This is up to a maximum of four. However, if a beneficiary is still considered a minor or where a life interest is involved, there should always be a minimum of two executors.

This is unless the testator appoints a trust corporation to administer the estate. Life interest refers to a gift that a person could only enjoy during his or her lifetime. After which, the gift goes to whoever the original donor has specified. This wouldn't be included in the person's estate to be disposed of.

Should there be only one executor where the beneficiary is still a minor or where a life interest is involved and until the estate is fully administrated, the courts may, on the guardian application or interested person, appoint in accordance to the rules of the court, one or more personal representation. This is in addition to the original personal representation, which is the executor.

(2) Renunciation Of Executorship

In instances where the executors appointed in the Will choose not to proceed with probate or in proving of the Will, they may choose to renounce their right. In these circumstances, they may choose to renounce their right to obtain the grant of probate.

When a person has renounced his right of obtaining a probate, he would normally be precluded from petitioning for probate. The court may, however, at its discretion, allow the person who has renounced his right to withdraw his renunciation. This happens when it is shown that the withdrawal would benefit the estate of those with an interest of the Will.

(3) Administrator

The person or trust corporation who is appointed by the court in the case of intestacy is called an administrator. An administrator might even be used when the person has died leaving a Will but didn't name an executor, or where the executor predeceased him.

Administrators may also be used if the executor refuses to proceed with the application of a grant of probate. The administrator derives his authority solely from the grant of the letters of administration and to validate the action that he may have to take, ought to extract the said grant.

When the order has been granted from the court, the person who petitioned for the order would need to get a seal copy of it from the court registry in order to carry out the term of the order. This process is referred to as the "extracting of the grant".

The maximum of four administrators may petition for letters of administration. In the case of executors where there is a minor beneficiary or life interest, the law would require a minimum of two individuals to be administrators. However, this exception to the requirement is when the trust corporation petitions for the grant of letters of administration. The need for a minimum of two administrators is dispensed of.

In the case of intestacy, the appointment of the personal representative is decided by the court. The court would decide who, among the beneficiaries, is best suited for the task.

There are different classes of entitled persons, in order of priority, to petition for letters of administration. If any person has a prior entitlement doesn't wish to apply for letters of administration, those who are entitled with a lower priority may proceed with the application. In such a situation, the person who has renounced his right would need to sign the relevant documents to this effect.

Once the court grants the letters of administration, it would have to regard the rights of all the persons interested in the estate of the deceased. As such, those persons who are entitled to petition for the letters of administration would include the spouse as well as the next of kin (of the intestate deceased).

There are some cases where the deceased may have left a Will appointing an executor but the executor isn't able to petition for the grant of probate. This may be because he is certified insane, handicapped, disabled, has migrated to another country or is dead.

There would also be certain cases where the testator has omitted the name of the executor in the Will. As such, the administration of the estate would need to be carried out with the Will annexed.

(4) Trustee

Generally, the function of a personal representative is to wind up the estate and distribute the assets while the function of the trustee is to hold up the assets until an event has happened. This event may be until a minor beneficiary has reached the age of majority. This is perhaps the most common.

In most situations, the testator would appoint the same person to be both the trustee and the executor. At times, the trust is created expressly by the Will but in many other times, it arises because of the operation of law. The operation of law occurs when there are minor beneficiaries and these gifts are not able to be distributed to them.

During this situation, there would be a normal progression from the role of a personal representative to that of a trustee. It isn't an easy task to decide the exact point in time that this transition would take place but for more practical reasons, it would have to be noted that once all the assets have been called in and vested in the personal representative, the trusteeship begins.

(5) Guardian

The scope of a Will isn't just limited to the disposal of the testator's estate. Having a guardian for the testator's children is also important, especially when the children are still considered a minor.

He may also appoint a guardian for the children in the event that the spouse predeceases him or even if both of them die together. This isn't an unusual circumstance as families would normally travel together.

In many situations, a Will would state the appointment of one or more guardians of "any of my infant children" to include children born after the date of the Will being written. If both the parents die, the appointed guardian would have the custody of the children and would be responsible for their health, support and education.

How To Choose An Executor

Without a doubt, it should be clear that the executor plays a very important role when it comes to administering the deceased's estate. It should be clear that due care is exercised when choosing a trustworthy and capable person to take on this responsibility. Among the issues you would need to consider include:

(1) Age Of The Executor

A consideration that has to be made is the age because if the executors in the Will were to die before the testator, the administration of the estate would need to be done by letters of administration with Will annexed. Therefore, an important thing to consider is how old your executors are.

If the testator is 35 years old but appoints someone who is 60 years old, there is a high possibility that the executor may pass on before the testator. Therefore, it is advisable to appoint someone who is younger than the testator.

(2) The Executor's Willingness And Capability To Act

This is perhaps the most important thing to consider. You would need to consider whether the executor is willing to act upon the death of the testator and capable of doing it.

This is because if no executor is available upon the testator's death, letters of administration with Will annexed would need to be applied instead of a grant of probate. The court would need to appoint a suitable person to the estate's administration. This would take much longer.

As such, it is important to obtain the consent of the person before his or her appointment as the executor. The duty of the testator is also to ensure that the person of his choice is capable - he shouldn't be mentally handicapped or insane, or have any clinical illness.

For many people, they may find that appointing their spouse as the executor very convenient. However, they should consider that it may not be very wise as the grieving spouse may not in a proper state of mind to deal with this demanding duties and complex procedures.

(3) Accountability And Integrity

For most people, their estate is what they have worked for during their whole lives. As such, when appointing an executor, he or she is entrusted the individual with a great responsibility in ensuring that the Will is being carried out. The executor would have the right to handle the deceased's affairs. To validate the authority of the executor, a grant of probate would need to be obtained first in order to deal with all the matters concerning to testator's estate.

As the executor has full access to the deceased's estate, there is a big possibility that he would be misusing or misappropriating the funds. To ensure that this doesn't happen, you would need to appoint someone with great integrity.

If the testator feels that the duties and responsibility of the executor is too much of a burden to his close ones or he may have problems appointing an executor because of a lack of trust, the better solution would be to appoint a trust corporation. This wouldn't burden other people who may elect against taking the responsibility of distributing the assets.

(4) Skills In Managing Assets

This is something that should be of main consideration as well, especially if the testator is someone with a lot of assets. In some circumstances, the executor's job may be to invest or ensure the continuation of the business. Therefore, having some financial or management knowledge, together with the ability to manage assets in such a manner would help generate income for that estate.

In most situations, the executors being appointed are working people who are very busy with their own jobs and lives as well. As such, they may not have time to administer the estate properly. They might also be not familiar with the procedures involves in extracting the grant of probate and the administration of the estate. This would delay the whole process and incur a lot of expenses.

As such, a trust corporation could be authorized to act as the executor, trustee and investment manager if required. The good thing about using a trust corporation is that it would assist you in as it wouldn't have the common problems of an individual executor like being incapable to act and having a limited existence (Trust corporations would not die).

Besides that, a trust corporation act in a more professional way and would be familiar with the common laws and procedures. This makes for a more efficient administration of the deceased's estate. However, the trust corporation's services would come with a fee and would also collect a percentage of the gross value of the estate.

The Personal Representative Responsibilities

When a person has left a Will, the responsibilities and duties of his personal representative would be laid down in the Will. This can be in addition to those which are being laid down by the relevant laws or when there is a variation or modification to the relevant clauses in those Acts. In this chapter are several important duties such as:-

(1) Locate The Will And Make Arrangements For The Funeral

Such duties would apply if the deceased dies testate while having a proved executor. A proved executor is someone who is willing and able to apply for probate. In such a circumstance, the executor being appointed would locate the Will and make all the funeral arrangement.

Some people may leave instructions in the Will with regards to the disposal of their bodies or the wish to donate certain organs to others or to medical research. This would be done by the executor as it is his or her responsibilities to ensure that the last wishes of the deceased are being carried out.

(2) Calling In The Assets

Another important duty of a personal representative is to decide the extent of the asset and liabilities of the deceased. To ensure this happens, an inquiry needs to be conducted thoroughly among the beneficiaries, his close friends and next of kin to ensure the actual value of his estate is determined. It may also involve writing to government department and financial institutions for details of the deceased's estate.

A Will is a great guide as to what the testator had owned but in many instances, not all the assets are being set out clearly in the Will. The testator may have decided to will away all his estate to a certain beneficiary or may have acquired additional assets after writing his Will.

If the estate is a large one, the responsibility of the personal representative becomes more difficult as it may also comprise certain other assets like jewelry, cash in the savings, property or shares. The deceased may even have certain assets overseas or assets in the name of the nominees.

There are also instances where the debtors owe the testator money. As such, if the testator, during his life, draw up an inventory of all his assets and their location would make the executor's work easier. The executor wouldn't need to go on a treasure hunt to find for all the assets.

The personal representatives need to act in a reasonable and diligently when it comes to the administration of the estate. Even if there isn't a time frame, the executor is expected to administer the estate expediently if he is running his own business.

One important thing to remember is that the burden imposed by the testator is on a normal person who has a lot of personal affairs to run. The executor might also be someone with no expertise whatsoever in the administration of the estate. This is a factor that should be always considered before there are any attempts to decide on his competence or efficiency in carrying out his responsibilities.

(3) Pay Off Debts And Liabilities

As said in the point above, there would be certain debts and liabilities in the testator's estate. They would need to be settled first before any assets can be distributed to the beneficiaries. Because of this, the beneficiaries would not be able to receive the full entitlement under the Will or anything at all if the estate is insolvent.

The personal representative or beneficiaries would not be personal liable for the deceased's debts and liabilities. The personal representative would only use the available assets of the estate to discharge the deceased's debts and liabilities.

In such an event that the estate is a huge one, it is advised for the personal representative to inform the creditors. They would need to invite them to submit a claim against the estate within a certain period. This is done through an advertisement placed in the Government Gazette or a newspaper.

In the stipulated period of time has lapsed, the personal representative may move to proceed with the distribution of assets. It is assumed that he is absolved of all liabilities that a claim is made after the expiry of the notice. However, it should be noted that individual creditors are still able to sue the estate for debts payment. The way of doing this is to merely trace the assets in the hand of the beneficiary or beneficiaries.

In this tough task, the personal representative would need to use his discretion to decide if an advertisement is needed to invite the creditors to submit their claims. This may not be relevant in smaller estates but for a medium or large estates, or when a testator is involved in business; it may be needed. To comply with the duties of a personal representative, advertisement are usually required so that all creditors who have any rights are discharged of his onus in carrying out the administration of the estate prudently and efficiently.

In general, the funeral expenses would need to be paid out first from the deceased's estate before the payment of any other debts or taxes. However, only reasonable funeral expenses are allowed. At times, the testator may have even left certain instructions in the Will concerning how he wants his liabilities and debts are paid.

It could also be noted in the Will that the testator can specify if he wants any particular beneficiary to have a priority. This means that his or her gift would not bear a burden in discharging the liabilities and debt. This is until and unless there isn't any available assets in the estate to settle those liabilities and debts.

(4) Be Impartial

Personal representative would need to be impartial in order to perform his duties. If it is proven that he has been biased by his actions, he could be sued by the beneficiary who is deeply affected by his actions.

(5) Distribution Of The Assets

Once the debts and liabilities are paid off, the remainder of the estate would need to be distributed to the beneficiaries. Once it is completed, the administration of the estate would cease.

If there has been a minor beneficiary or a life interest, this personal representative would also take on the role of a trustee if he or she is appointed as a trustee under the Will. The trustee would administer the estate until the minor reaches the age of majority or until the death of the beneficiary of the life interest.

At times, the testator may decide that a gift be held in trust for a beneficiary beyond the age of majority. For such a case, the administration of the estate wouldn't be completed until the trust ends. If the testator has appointed a different person to be trustee, the personal representative would need to transfer the said assets to the trustee after the payment of all debts and liabilities.

(6) Accounting For The Estate

Before distributing the assets to the beneficiaries, the personal representative would need to submit accounts to the beneficiaries for their personal use and approval.

As a matter of fact, during the administration of the estate, the personal representative has the duty of rendering proper accounts to a beneficiary who demands for it. It is prudent for the personal representative to ensure that proper accounts are being kept the moment he starts to administer the estate. It wouldn't need to be audited unless there is a dispute or court order for it to be audited properly.

The Trustee's Power

The trustee is given powers to carry out his or her duties. However, there are certain situations where the testator could give his trustee additional powers above what is provided by the act.

A good example of extra powers that a testator could give to his trustee is the power to continue the testator's business. As no such power is given to the trustee, the trustee would act on his own risk if he carries out the business and he might be liable for any debts which are being incurred. In most situations, if such power isn't accorded to him, the trustee would wind up the business and divide the proceeds among the beneficiaries.

The trustee could also seek professional advice during the administration of the estate. This includes advice provided by the lawyer, accountant or investing consultant. However, because the trustee has a duty to ensure that competent people are employed, the trustee may be liable for any losses suffered. As such, the trustee should exercise diligence and due care when it comes to the appointment of such professional agents.

Chapter 12 - Checklist Before Preparing Your Will

From what you have read, I am sure you have understood why writing a Will is so important. It should also be clear that there are many things which you need to consider before you start writing one.

This is a simple checklist which you should have before you start writing your Will. Make sure you have everything checked first as it will help you with everything.

✓ **Your Executors**. Write down the names of your executors and see if they are the right people to assist you. Are they trustyworthy and responsible? Seek permission from them before you appoint them. Make sure that you get their names, personal details and address accurate as these are important information.

✓ **A Proper Guardian**. Find a person who could be the guardian for your minor children (if you have them) and seek their permission. Then, get their names, personal details and address accurate. This is similar to finding your executors.

✓ **The Beneficiaries**. List down all the beneficiaries to your will together with the particulars.

✓ **Your Assets**. Write down all the assets that you have. Take special notice on the bigger items or valuable belongings like your land, property and car. You also need to list other items such as your savings, fixed deposit or jewelry.

- ✓ **Who Should Receive What**. Select the beneficiary and decide what he or she should have. The division should be clearly defined to ensure that there are no quarrels among the beneficiaries.

- ✓ **Special Instructions And Terms of Endearment**. These can be included in the Will. This may also include special instructions regarding how you want your funeral to be conducted or the loving messages to your loved one. If you want to ensure that this is included, special drafts have to be prepared to follow your instructions.

The moment you have considered all these details, you are now able to instruct your Will-writer to prepare your Will. With all these information in place, writing a will would be much easier.

Chapter 13 - In The Event Of Death

In the event that a person passes away, the very first thing that the family member would need to do is to check if there is a Will being left behind by the deceased. This can be very difficult if the deceased has never talked about it during his or her lifetime.

Therefore, it is prudent practice to inform someone about your Will the moment you have written one. Tell that person about it and indicate where your Will is being kept. If no one is aware of any Will being made, the family members would have to apply for letters of administration and your estate would be distributed according to the legislation.

In my experience, there has been certain cases where Wills have been suppressed because they were kept by people who may not have been adequately provided for or been discriminated against. As such, you shouldn't only let someone know you have written a Will, but also ensure that it is in a safe place where it could be retrieved easily without the fears of being tampered with.

As it is ascertained whether there is a Will, the appropriate letters of representation would need to be petitioned for.

Testacy - Grant Of Probate

The steps to petition for a probate:

Preliminary Steps:

- **Obtain Extract Of Death Certificate**. This is obtained at the Registrar of Births and Deaths, after filing with the court. Together with the copy of the original Wills, it should be attached to the petition and filed in court.

- **Obtain A Translation**. If the Will is another foreign language, a certified true translation would need to be obtained and attached. A competent person in the language would need to translate the Will. His competence in the language should also be clearly stated in the translation.

Procedures:

- Petition has to be verified on oath by the executor.
- If there has been a delay in the petition made (normally after three years), the reason for delay should be clearly set out in the petition.
- If there has been no attestation clause (a statement in the Will that it has been duly executed in the presence of a witness) or where the clause is inadequate, the Registrar would need an affidavit of due execution. It should be from at least one attesting witness or any person present during the time of execution. If such a person cannot be obtained, the Registrar might accept the signature of the Will as the handwriting of the deceased.

- Once the grant is approved, the executor would have to extract it.

Intestacy - Letters Of Administration

The process of petitioning for letters of administration:

(1) Procedure In Appointment Of Administrator

This petition would be filed by a beneficiary who has the priority over other beneficiary. Every other beneficiary should renounce his right to petition and sign a letter called the renunciation of administration. If this is not done yet, a notice should be served on those people who refuse to sign when the petition comes up for hearing. If there is someone who wants to object, he could do so and the petition would be considered a contentious one. However, if he doesn't appear during the hearing, he is deemed to have renounced his right to administration.

(2) Administration Bond

Before the grant of letters of administration can be extracted, an administration bond would first be required. This is a form of security before the deceased's estate can be administrated. This means that the administrator must get two sureties to sign the bond before the grant can be extracted.

The sureties must also sign the bond before the grant can be extracted and must have assets within the jurisdiction and ensure that the property would be administered properly and the accounts rendered properly.

The court can decide to decrease the number of sureties, dispense them or reduce the amount of the bond. Sureties can be dispensed with if a trust corporation is appointed as the administrator or if the administrator is considered the sole beneficiary.

Letters of Administration with Will Annexed

There are situations where a person dies with a proper and valid Will and a grant of probate isn't petition for, but letters of administration are used instead. This is because occasionally, the person is named as executor in the Will, for certain reasons, and is unable to petition for a probate. During these cases, the executor may:

- Predeceased the testator
- Be insane or suffer from certain critical illness or handicap
- Died after the testator but before proving the Will
- Be a resident outside the local jurisdiction
- Did not come forward to petition

In certain cases, a valid Will would have been executed but the testator may have completely overlooked the naming of an executor. For such a case, the similar procedure of intestacy would apply but the Will would need to be annexed to demonstrate the testator's intention for the estate distribution.

The individual who can file a petition for letters of administration with Will annexed would be the similar person entitled under the rules of priority for letters of administration.

Administration De Bonis Non

Such a situation would arise when the person who has taken out the probate or letters of administration hasn't completed the administration of the estate due to:

- Incapacity
- Death
- Abscondment

"Administration De Bonis Non" involves the similar procedure as obtaining any letters of administration and could only be made to the persons entitled to the original grant.

This generally means that the person who has the rights to file for a petition for letters in this category would again be the person who is entitled under the rules of priority for letter of administration. Therefore, Administration De Bonis Non acts under the Will of the deceased in the case of testacy.

However, if the estate is an intestate one, the authority he derives comes from the appointment as administrator and as he carries out the functions of his predecessor. In such a case, the role of the administrator is strictly restricted to finalizing the estate's administration.

Chapter 14 - Checking The Different Legislation

All the information that you read in this book may not represent a worldwide view with regards to Wills. Wills are governed by the different legislations in different countries. Therefore, you would have to check the different legislation in the country you are in before you prepare your Will.

However, the information in this book is a great step to understanding the topic. You would be more equipped to write a Will and understand what to prepare before you look for a Will writer. Do take all the effort required to check your local legislation before you start preparing your Will.

Visit: http://Wills.wellbeingvalley.com/

Resource - Want A Will Written For You?

From this book, I'm sure that you know the importance of having a Will.

Do you want to get a Will written now?

You can get it online using this amazing *Wills and Estate Planning forms*. It would provide you with state specific Wills, Testament forms and other Estate Planning Documents **at a fraction of the price charged by an attorney**.

Protect your family and assets now!

Visit: http://Wills.wellbeingvalley.com/

Don't waste the money on having expensive attorney when you can get quality forms. Get your Will written easily now. Not only that - you get to ensure your privacy.

Visit this link immediately:

http://Wills.wellbeingvalley.com/

www.ingramcontent.com/pod-product-compliance
Lightning Source LLC
Chambersburg PA
CBHW051331170526
45166CB00002B/762